# Burscough Bo

Their marriages and t.......

Robert Cheetham-Houghton

First Published 1998 by Countyvise, 14 Appin Road, Birkenhead, Wirral, Merseyside L41 9HH.

Copyright ©1998 Robert Cheetham-Houghton

British Library Cataloguing in Publication Data.
A catalogue record for this book is available from the British Library.

ISBN 1 901231 12 7

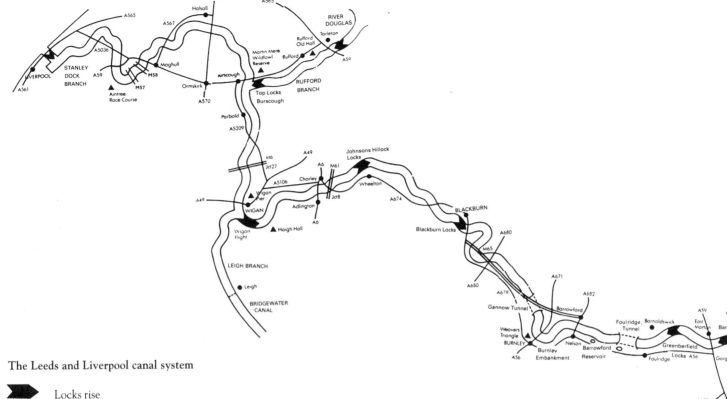

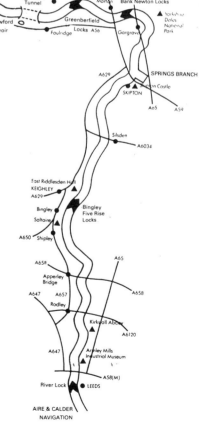

## The Leeds and Liverpool canal system

 Locks rise

There are 91 locks in all on the Liverpool to Leeds canal route.
Forty-six of them rise from Liverpool. The first one encountered is
Appley Lock near Appley Bridge, Wigan. The summit is at
Greenberfield when the remaining 45 locks fall to Leeds.

| | |
|---|---|
| Liverpool to Bootle | 4 miles |
| Bootle to Burscough Bridge | 20 1/4 miles |
| Burscough to Wigan | 11 miles |
| Wigan to Blackburn | 22 miles |
| Blackburn to Burnley | 16 miles |
| Burnley to Nelson | 6 miles |
| Nelson to Skipton | 19 miles |
| Skipton to Keighley | 11 miles |
| Keighley to Shipley | 6 miles |
| Total distance | 127 1/4 miles |

The distance via the public highway is 75 miles. On the canal the
speed limit is 4 mph, at an average of 2 1/2 mph on account of time
lost negotiating the locks.

The full carrying capacity of a 62ft x 14ft motor boat is 55 tonnes,
although bulk baled wool cargo and the like can be much less.

**Acknowledgements**

My thanks to Bob Goldborough, Liverpool artist, who painted to perfection the front cover, solely from a verbal description from my imagination.

My thanks also to Mrs Hilda Watkinson, widow and ex-boatwoman, now in her nineties and living in retirement alongside the canal at Burnley, for the provision of many of the photographs. And to Douglas Moore Ltd (boatbuilders), Summit Pound, Barnoldswick.

For any further information on the contents of this book, the author can be contacted on 0151 226 2540, or at 8B Abingdon Grove, Walton Hall, Liverpool L4 9UY.

Book design by:
March Design
Liverpool

The author aged six in 1930, by Litherland Gasworks wall, Bootle-cum-Linacre

# Burscough Boatmen

Their marriages and their boats

Robert Cheetham-Houghton

# Burscough Boatmen

This book is presented as a record and a sort of 'Roll of Honour' to the men and women, their loves and their marriages, who navigated the 14ft wide by 62ft long boats along the stretches and scenic miles of the Leeds and Liverpool Canal, in all kinds of weather and for such a long time. It is to immortalise the memory of the boatmen of Burscough town, West Lancashire. These people, as the reader will come to realise, were a unique community with their own special characteristics, customs and way of life. They were the first people to crew and work the barges along the initial completed lengths of waterway from Liverpool to Wigan, and on completion, all the way to the city of Leeds.

The first sod of the canal was cut at the start of the making of the 127 1/4-mile waterway route at Halsall, near Ormskirk, in 1770, just a few miles from Burscough. It was literally cut out manually, with barrows and spades, by a workforce that consisted mostly of Irish immigrant navvies (the word 'navvie' being an abbreviation for navigational accomplishments by construction).

Boat people, both male and female, were a very hardy and resourceful breed. They had to be, to be able to follow an occupation that required them to live aboard barges in very cramped cabins and in a crude and exposed environment. They washed in heated canal water using the carbolic soap of the times, which appeared to do their health and complexions no harm whatsoever. Their other toilet facilities and functions were generally behind a hedgerow alongside the towpath, or the use of a bucket in an empty hold, or in the forrid (forward) cabin, which was then emptied into the canal at an opportune time and place. Between themselves, the women also mastered the art of midwifery when an increase in the family was due.

Before the turn of the century, the majority of boat people, like others, were partially or totally illiterate, as were both my parents, and I think this was a contributing factor to the reason why they were always ready to help each other, especially when unforeseen navigational problems arose, causing delay, and other reasons. Their attitude was always one of: 'There but for the grace of God …'

Sons and daughters of boatmen rarely married outside their own closely knit community, and for generation after generation they named their children constantly and repetitively, both male and female, with just one Christian name, using very few different names in comparison to their numbers.

From a compilation of almost 700 marriages that took place among them between the 1840s and 1930s, of the males or bridegrooms, 103 were named William, 98 John, 88 Thomas, 84 James, 37 Richard, and 42 Robert. Of the brides, 78 were named Elizabeth, 70 Ellen, 70 Mary, 69 Margaret, 50 Ann, Anne or Annie, 37 Jane, 35 Alice, and lots of Catherines and Sarahs. In this book, some individuals may be recorded more than once, because of widowhood or re-marriage.

The boats they worked and lived aboard were gaily painted with many flowery scrolls and designs comparable with gipsy caravans, both inside the cabins and the exterior, including the wooden fresh-water cask, which was always kept on the stern 'live-in' cabin deck. In fact, bargees could aptly be described as 'water gipsies'.

By the middle of the 1880s, whole families were living and actively helping to work the boats, some members starting when they were as young as eight years of age by learning to steer the the boats, running ahead of them along the towpath to turn off the many wooden swing bridges along the route, helping to fill the fresh-water cask by carrying the water from an available horse stable tap, and doing numerous other necessary jobs within their young ability. Some boatmen were still working when they were past eighty years old.

Over the years, there were a number of accidents which caused premature deaths among families, the most prevalent being drowning. This happened mostly when locks were being operated and someone fell into the lock when sluice gates were open, or they were crushed between the lock wall and the boat.

One accident in the 1920s left a boatwoman with a severed leg: the boat was being discharged at the Tate & Lyle unloading berths, which were situated between Chisenhale and Burlington Street. The chain holding the crane grab, used for scooping out cargoes of coal from the hold, snapped, causing the grab to fall and crash onto the stern deck, through the timbers and partly into the living-in cabin where Lizzie (Elizabeth) Jackson, wife of Richard Jackson, was sitting. She recovered in a Liverpool hospital and was very lucky not to have been killed. Eventually she was awarded £800 damages with costs against the sugar refiners and retired to a bungalow in Parbold, which she purchased with some of the money. Despite her horrific accident, Lizzie Jackson, nee Watkinson, lived to be 93 years old. She died in 1991 and is interred at Christchurch Douglas churchyard on Parbold Hill.

This information was related to me by her sister-in-law Hilda Watkinson, nee Foster, a boatwoman all her working life. She started when she was a very young girl, which interrupted her schooling somewhat. Hilda was born in 1905 at Ring O' Bells, Lathom, near Burscough, where a lot of boat people hailed from. Her father was Thomas Foster, a boatman who owned four boats on the canal. Hilda too is now in retirement, aged 93, and living alongside the canal in Burnley.

Boating was all piece work with no regular hours or days to work, or holiday pay, etc. It was a seven-day involvement. In the days of the horse-boat, the captain was the only member of the crew who was paid by the boat owners; it was called 'freight money' or 'tonnage'. It was paid for what cargo had been carried, the distance travelled, and was paid only when the goods had been delivered.

With the money received the captain paid the mate, who was most probably a member of the family, perhaps the captain's wife or son. He also had to pay for all the other incidentals like fodder for the horse, stabling charges, replacement ropes and tackle, in fact for everything necessary to operate the boat and sustain the family. The only concession he enjoyed was to have sufficient coal (part of the cargo carried) for the two cabin stove fires, one at the bow and the other at the stern end, on which all cooking was done and water boiled. The coal was unofficial, of course, with nothing in writing, but the practice was ignored and coal was a cheap commodity in those days.

The general rule was: no cargo delivered, no payment of wages due. There was no compensation for unavoidable delays, like when the canal froze over, insufficient water depth caused through drought or leakage, fog, or perhaps the horse feeling unwell, going lame or even suddenly dropping dead (which happened occasionally through age or overwork). Boat owners supplied the boat to be towed, subsequent repairs, but not the horse or anything else. In later years, around the 1930s, when steam-, then diesel-driven timber and steel-plated boats came into being, both the captain and the mate, by now all male, were in the employ of the owners and were paid by them. They also supplied everything else for the running of the craft: fuel oil, ropes, tackle, etc.

The matrimonial activities of the larger 40 or so boat families has resulted, over a period of over a hundred years, in them being related to each other in one form or another. On a number of occasions, marriages took place in which the bride did not change her maiden name, for example when first cousins, like brothers' sons and daughters married each other. Today, I would estimate that 80 per cent of the last generation of Burscough boatmen and women are interred in the churchyard of St John the Baptist, Burscough, the place where a large number of them were also married. Leeds and Liverpool Canal boat people now in retirement will eventually become a totally extinct breed. Another unique fact about them is the closeness they enjoyed and sustained in their working life. In a way it still remains even after death; many of my seniors are laid to rest in graves that are often side by side in St John's. They are now resting in peace with no worries of weather conditions, or the state of health of their only means of working locomotion, the boat horse. The horse will have pulled them from one destination to another, through some very foul and fair elements, and for countless miles at a sometimes monotonous pace. The horse was part of the family and to look after his or her wellbeing was a very essential part of all the operations.

Since the final closure to commercial traffic on the Leeds and Liverpool Canal some 30 years ago, many books and photographs have been published about it, but none about the people who worked on it. They didn't mix with land-lubbers to a great extent. This inland waterway which operated for two hundred years and carried a far greater tonnage than any other canal in Britain, now lies almost derelict along its many miles, including the branches off at Burscough to Rufford (Rufford Line) near Preston, and the branch at Wigan to Leigh and Manchester, where it becomes the Bridgewater Canal, affectionately called Dukes' Cut by boatmen, after the man who gave it his name, the Duke of Bridgewater.

The success of the canal's carrying capacity was made possible because of its initial wide construction, allowing 14ft-wide boats to navigate its cutting and to negotiate the wide locks, in comparison to other British barge canals. The countless narrow boats you see today, invariably converted into house barges or pleasure craft and moored alongside its banks never operated commercially on the L & L Canal and were seldom seen on it. Narrow boats sailed on the narrow waterways with similarly constructed locks in Wales, the Midlands and the South of England.

One of the reasons why the majority of boating families hailed from Burscough town or thereabouts was because the Canal Company first set up a depot and headquarters there and a lot of recruitment in the early 1800s for canal workers and crews commenced at Burscough. From then on, fathers, sons, daughters and indeed whole families participated in the work and special way of life, living on the boats. Some of them were born in the cabins. It brought into being because of their numbers, acquired skills and place of origin, the description of being 'Burscough Boatmen'.

To give an insight into the very close relationship which existed between them, I have researched and complied, with a lot of personal sentiment, a list of almost 700 marriages that took place among them between 1837 and 1935. This too is a unique record, for the reason that these marriages took place in only a few churches. Some of them were situated in the Parish of Liverpool, St Johns, Burscough, St Cuthberts at Halsall, Christchurch Douglas, Parbold, with just one marriage at the ancient parish church of All Saints, Wigan. This was between Thomas Bowen and Ann Grimshaw in 1890.

Unlike the majority of other boat people of her generation, Ann Bowen could read and write, not so husband Tom. For a number of years they lived in retirement on the canalside at Appley Lock Cottages, Appley Bridge, near Parbold, until they died (Ann first) within 12 months of each other in 1949 and 1950 having been married for almost 60 years, and having spent the whole of their working life on the canal, working a horse-drawn boat. They too, along with other boatmen, are buried on Parbold Hill which overlooks the canal.

The majority of bargees who married in Liverpool did so at the Parish Church of Our Lady and St Nicholas, in Chapel Street by the Pier Head, known in times past as the 'sailors' church' because of its frequent use by members of ships' crews from the nearby docks. My great great grandfather, James Cheetham, was a boatman, or a 'waterman' as they were earlier described. He was born in Halsall in 1794; his son, John, my great grandfather, was also born in Halsall in 1817; then his son Henry, my grandfather, was born there in 1845. Although about half of boatmen's marriages took place in Liverpool, very few of them resided in the parish. Before the turn of the last century, whole families lived, worked and slept aboard the boats which were fitted out with cabin bunks, cupboards, a pull-down table and a small stove fire to cook meals on.

When bargees married in Liverpool, they gave their place of residence briefly as Pall Mall, Leeds Street or Vauxhall Road: these were the locations where the boats they lived on were moored at the time of their marriages. Pall Mall and Leeds Street was the address of the head office of Canal Transport Ltd., who owned the majority of the boats which carried cargoes the full length of the canal.

Vauxhall Road was the boat berths of Tate & Lyle sugar refinery and the two Liverpool Gas Works, one in Eccles Street and the other in Athol Street, both off Vauxhall Road. These were also the main depots where cargoes of coal, sugar, wool, machinery and miscellaneous merchandise were brought to and taken from the city and port.

I have surmised that the addresses given at their weddings were to make them more acceptable to the clergy of Liverpool, who would marry the couples from 'up country' who lived on floating homes. The main reason why boat people chose to marry in Liverpool was mainly one of convenience. The then thriving port was the principal destination for canal traffic, the coal brought into the city from the Wigan coalfields was to feed factory furnaces, in the process of refining sugar and for making domestic gas. A lot of the cargoes of machinery and other commodities were for export via the Liverpool docks. Thousands of tonnes of baled wool and refined sugar were transported yearly from the two Canal Transport warehouses, one at Bootle and from Tate & Lyle's, to the numerous mill towns and cities of Lancashire and Yorkshire.

It was when boat crews had a day or more of waiting to load or discharge these cargoes in the Vauxhall Road area, that they took the opportunity to walk to the churches to keep pre-arranged appointments to get 'spliced' (married).

To get to the Liverpool Parish church the wedding party would either walk the mile or so, or take a tramcar ride along Vauxhall Road, turning into Tithebarn Street, passing the then Exchange Railway Station and down into Chapel Street. As I recall, in the 1930s it was a number 16 Liverpool Corporation tram, Litherland to the Pier Head, which served the area.

These wedding parties would be made up of the bride and bridegroom, the best man and a witness, probably from other boat crews. All would be clad in their Sunday best and wearing the traditional boatmen's garb which comprised the wearing of clogs, by both males and females, with the footwear most probably having had goose grease applied to them to give them a polished look, at the same time making the hardwearing leather uppers a little more supple, as they clattered their way along Liverpool street pavements and up the stone steps leading to the church. Most of the men would have been wearing khaki-coloured corduroy trousers and a hand-knitted, dark navy blue 'gansey' (jersey). A spotted necker-chief was invariably worn around the neck and knotted at the throat. Some of the men wore flat cloth caps as Sunday best, but most donned trilby hats without the dent in the centre, and with a lowered brim all around, to give protection from the wind and the rain when working the boat. Gold earrings, possibly handed down family heirlooms, were worn by a number of both sexes. The boatwomen wore ankle-length skirts, shawls, and head bonnets tied under the chin. Their universal mode of dress made boat people instantly recognisable to townspeople.

On the odd occasion when the two witnesses necessary for the marriage might not be available, a church warden would be asked to oblige and add his signature to the marriage certificate. Before the 1890s and because of the illiteracy of many boatmen and women (this is borne out by the many Xs, their mark, as signatures on certificates) many official copies contain misspelt surnames, e.g. Aughton for Houghton, Kilshaw for Culshaw, Gobbin for Gibbons, Deacon instead of Deakin, etc. In my compilations I have corrected some of the obvious mistakes known to me. (For people who seek to research their family trees and who rely on records in alphabetical order, these errors make it much more difficult to do so.) The factors which could have caused the spelling mistakes in these instances might have been because of the inability of some boat people to spell out their own name, or perhaps the broad Lancashire accent was not readily understood and decoded by some of the Liverpool clergy.

In the late 1880s, when boatmen started to acquire houses – some especially built for them and their families, houses which are still tenented to this day, in Burscough town itself and at places nearby, such as Canal Bank, New Lane – the women began to remain at home while sons continued to act as mates to their fathers, and the younger children started to attend the now compulsory schooling. By the 1940s there were very few wives working the boats with their husbands, and the horse-towed type were gradually being replaced by both timber and steel-plated, diesel engine powered craft.

Canal Transport Ltd. named most of their timber-built boats after planets, and the iron boats after British rivers.

The ending of the war in 1945 and the eventual construction of motorways sealed the fate for canals generally. From then onwards, boat captains, their sons and mates started to leave the Romany piece-work way of life for other types of better paid work, with guaranteed hours and wages – jobs that enabled them to be at home each night. They chose jobs on the land, the railway and factory work. Quite a number went to work in ordnance depots situated at Burscough and nearby Chorley.

The completion of motorways heralded the final blow to inland waterways; canal transport had become too slow and uneconomical. Today, the giant Tate & Lyle sugar refinery and the two gasworks in Liverpool, which required hundreds of tonnes of coal to be delivered by canal barges each week, are no more. Most of the Vauxhall Road industrial area has been bulldozed and replaced by dwelling houses. There is very little left to show the abundance of commercial activity that was once prevalent. The umpteen small 'open all hours' shops where boat people purchased essentials in preparation for setting off 'up cut' once more, and which catered also for the thousands of other workers employed in the area, have all gone. Even the original terminus of the Leeds and Liverpool Canal, the stretch that ran parallel to Pall Mall and the location of Canal Transport's head office and warehouses has now been filled in and built upon.

From being one of the youngest recruits to the canal in 1938, thus following in the ways of my ancestors, I am now becoming one of the oldest in retirement. There are still many older than myself and well into their eighties, with a few in their nineties. On a warm and sunny summer's day, some old boatmen can be seen at various locations alongside the canal, or sitting on benches set on pavements on the main road that passes through Burscough Bridge (to Preston in one direction and Liverpool in the other), probably reminiscing about their working life.

Today, over half a century later, the children and grandchildren of past boatmen and women have different occupations and wider horizons. With the advent of the car and other modes of transport, larger towns and places which once seemed remote and a good way away have now become more easily accessible.

This new generation now marry outside their once close-knit community. They can all read and write, indeed some are business people and academics. They choose a greater variety of Christian names for their children, and some are earning their living in far away places like Australia and New Zealand. This is a stark contrast to their parents and grandparents who rarely ventured further than a canalside tavern, a nearby fish and chip shop, or to pay a visit to the many music halls and picture houses that abounded in Liverpool (such as the Rotunda in Scotland Road, Liverpool, the Metropole, Bootle, also the Hippodrome, King Street, Wigan) and Leeds city, and all other Lancashire and Yorkshire berths where they happened to be tied up for the night.

The canal's water still flows along its lengths and under its bridges, but for those of us still remaining, it flows now carrying only cargoes of memories and the ghosts of a very special family of people. Their like will never be seen again.

# Burscough Boatmen and Women
# Marriages 1837 - 1935

**The majority of names that constituted Burscough boatmen 1770-1935**
Abram, Alty, Ashcroft, Ashton, Aspinall, Baldwin, Barrow, Baybutt, Bentham, Blinkhorn, Blundell, Bowen, Bridge, Carrington, Caunce, Cheetham, Culshaw, Dakin, Deakin, Disley, Draper, Dutton, Fazakerley, Foreshaw, Gibbons, Gill, Glover, Gore, Gregson, Grimshaw, Halsall, Harrison, Hartley, Hesketh, Howard, Howcroft, Hunter, Jackson, Lamb, Langton, Lawson, Lea, Mawdsley, Melling, Parr, Peet, Prescot, Pye, Reynolds, Robinson, Ruddock, Sharrock, Shaw, Smith, Snape, Spencer, Swift, Tasker, Taylor, Thompson, Turner, Tyrer, Varley, Vickers, Walker, Wareing, Watkinson, Webster, Wright.

**1837**
James Prescott — Ann Wilso
James Snape *Wid* — Hannah Spencer *Wid*
**1839**
William Ashton — Ellen Hartley
**1840**
John Cheetham — Mary Shaw
Richard Fazakerley — Mary Johnson
**1841**
Thomas Shaw — Ellen Taylor
William Wright — Lucy Lamb
**1846**
Henry Deakin — Margaret Gill
Robert Halsall — Betty Gill

**1847**
George Shaw — Elizabeth Forshaw
**1848**
William Sharrock — Maria O'Rourke
**1849**
John Aspinall — Mary Draper *Wid*
Robert Evans — Ellen Weedall
John Aspinall — Jane Fairclough
James Carrington — Mary Halsall
Richard Rimmer — Esther Green
Thomas Robinson — Mary A Cheetham
Thomas Sharman — Margaret Worthington
William Wright — Margaret Eccleston *Wid*
**1850**
Thomas Thompson — Ann Worthington
John Wareing — Ellen Dutton
**1851**
John Currie — Catherine Baldwin
Henry Gill — Eleanor Hesketh
John Harrison — Catherine Jackson
James Prescott — Margaret Cheetham
John Spencer — Ellen Turner
James Wittacker — Eleanor Thompson
**1852**
William Ashcroft — Elizabeth Harrison
Thomas Halsall — Alice Close *Wid*
Thomas Hartley — Catherine Shaw
Thomas Robinson — Sarah Culshaw *Wid*
William Sharrock — Alice Banks
Henry Simms — Hannah Bridge
Robert Spencer — Ann Close
John Snape — Ann Howcroft
Thomas Webster — Elizabeth Lamb
Thomas Wright — Sarah Ann Horsefield
**1853**
John Hesketh — Ann Atherton

James Horrocks — Susannah Smith
William Howard — Ann Forshaw
Robert Howcroft — Elizabeth Spencer
George Lawson — Martha Lawson
James Sharrock — Elizabeth Waterworth
James Snape — Elizabeth Howcroft
**1854**
Henry Draper — Ellen Pemberton
James Draper — Ellen Barton
Thomas Tyrer — Margaret Tiomey
**1855**
Henry Harrison — Ellen Langton
James Johnson — Ann Bridge
Robert Prescott — Ann Fairhurst
Robert Snape — Sarah Harrison
Edward Thompson — Mary Carrington
**1856**
Adam Ashcroft — Mary Ann Eccles
Stephen Aspinall — Margaret Rothwell
James Barrow — Susan Howard
Thomas Culshaw — Ann Deakin
Thomas Fazakerley — Alice Banks
William Gill — Ann Jackson
William Melling — Mary Shaw
John Peet — Margaret Gill
Thomas Prescott — Margaret Parr
William Sharrock — Jane Hurst
Henry Smith — Mary Duckworth
Lewis Taylor — Alice Ashcroft
**1857**
Thomas Alty — Margaret Harrison
James Aspinall — Alice Hornby
Johnathon Carrington — Mary Jackson
Richard Dakin — Elizabeth Sharrock
John Dobson — Ellen Fazakerley
James Howard — Mary Blundell

Robert Lamb — Mary Forshaw
James Spencer — Elizabeth Turner
**1858**
Edward Aspinall — Elizabeth Alty
Henry Blundell *Wid* — Mary Eaves
Henry Cheetham — Ann Dobson
Thomas Hartley — Alice Robinson
John Lea — Elizabeth Baldwin
James Reynolds — Ann Robinson
Henry Robinson — Ellen Cottier *Wid*
William Robinson — Alice Rothwell
Ellen Prescott — William Robinson
Daniel Vickers — Mary Lawson
**1859**
William Denton — Jane Rimmer
Thomas Gill — Lydia Lamb
Thomas Gough — Jane Shaw
John Grimshaw — Mary Ann Montgomery
John Harrison — Jane Halsall
William Harrison — Ellen Stringfellow
Luke Hunter — Mary Disley
William Hartley — Margaret Jackson
John Melling — Jane Howard
Thomas Melling — Jane Lea
**1860**
James Barrow — Mary Robinson
William Draper — Elizabeth Harrison
James Gaskell — Elizabeth Woodward
Peter Harrison — Margaret Draper
John Hornby — Mary Seddon
Thomas Snape — Catherine Mawdsley
**1861**
Henry Bamber — Julia Denton
James Cheetham — Cecily Johnson
Robert Gore — Alice Shaw
David Gill — Ellen Lamb

| | |
|---|---|
| William Jones | Ann Tyrer |
| John Smith | Elizabeth Ashcroft |
| Richard Smith | Alice Carrington |
| John Fred Walker | Ellen Barnes |
| Robert Wareing | Maria Edmondson |
| William Watkinson | Mary Culshaw |

**1862**

| | |
|---|---|
| Frederick Bentham | Esther Green |
| Thomas Draper | Mary Lamb |
| John Sharrock | Ann Waterworth |
| James Smith | Margaret Bateman |
| John Spencer | Esther Ratcliffe |
| William Turner | Jane Worthington |
| John Wareing | Ann Howard |
| Henry Watkinson | Jane Johnson |

**1863**

| | |
|---|---|
| William Baldwin *Wid* | Ann Sutton |
| Fairhurst Baybutt | Elizabeth Cheetham |
| George Dobson | Elizabeth Gibbons |
| Thomas Forshaw | Margaret Smith |
| William Forshaw | Isabella Hesketh |
| Peter Gibbons | Jane Disley |
| George Gibbons | Jane Halsall |
| William Lamb | Sarah Lawson *Wid* |
| George Peet | Sarah Cheetham |
| Richard Seddon | Alice Mawdsley |
| John Shaw | Mary Ellen Bryan |
| William Shaw | Alice Maddocks |

**1864**

| | |
|---|---|
| John Barrow | Mary Taylor *Wid* |
| Robert Dakin | Alice Parkinson |
| John Denton | Elizabeth Hunter |
| Owen Evans | Jane Draper *Wid* |
| Thomas Forshaw | Alice Spencer |
| John Gregson | Lydia Denton |
| Richard Jackson | Susan Hesketh |
| William Jackson | Catherine Pedder |
| James Jones *Wid* | Margaret Sharman *Wid* |
| James S Lamb *Wid* | Mary Culshaw *Wid* |
| John Lawson | Catherine Greenhall *Wid* |
| James Robinson | Martha Pye |
| James Rothwell | Margaret Disley |
| William Smith | Ellen Melling |

| | |
|---|---|
| Thomas Spencer | Martha Ashcroft |
| Richard Turner | Elizabeth Blundell |
| Robert Waterworth | Charlotte Dawson |

**1865**

| | |
|---|---|
| James Aspinall | Eliza Watson |
| Thomas Aspinall | Martha Flitcroft |
| John Bentham | Sarah Gaskell |
| James Carrington | Alice Jackson |
| William Cartmell | Jane Caunce |
| James Disley | Jane Culshaw |
| Thomas Disley | Ann Shaw |
| John Harrison | Esther Langton |
| William Hewitt | Kate Plumb |
| Robert Howard | Margaret Smith |
| James Plumb | Ann Hind |
| William Wilson Price | Margaret Forshaw *Wid* |
| Robert Spencer | Ann Rimmer |

**1866**

| | |
|---|---|
| James Bentham | Elizabeth Thompson |
| James Carrington | Margaret Taylor |
| Henry Cheetham | Catherine Carrington |
| James Dutton | Winifred Watkinson |
| Richard Dutton | Alice Barrow |
| Henry Eaves | Hannah Thompson |
| James Forshaw | Elizabeth Carrington |
| Richard Forshaw | Mary Foster |
| Job Gore | Alice Forshaw |
| Richard Hesketh | Ann Prescott *Wid* |
| Stephen Lamb | Mary Lawson |
| John Lawson | Emma Shaw |
| William Nuttall | Alice Ashton |
| Robert Smith | Ellen Irlern |
| Thomas Tyrer *Wid* | Harriet Ormanly |
| Richard Webster | Sarah Hartley |
| William Webster | Isobella Smith |
| John Worthington | Benigna Lamb |

**1867**

| | |
|---|---|
| Robert Alty | Ann Smith |
| James Baldwin | Susannah Gregson |
| James Carrington | Mary Rimmer |
| Henry Disley | Ellen Hunter |
| James Dutton *Wid* | Hannah Spencer |
| John Eccleston | Naome Disley |

| | |
|---|---|
| Henry Forshaw | Margaret Ollerton |
| John Hilton | Jane Watkinson |
| James Prescott *Wid* | Jane Ashcroft |
| James Robinson | Eliza Harrison |
| Henry Robinson | Martha Sharrock |
| John Sharrock *Wid* | Marion Speed |
| William Thompson *Wid* | Elizabeth Conner *Wid* |

**1868**

| | |
|---|---|
| Richard Aspinall | Alice Gill |
| Henry Howcroft | Sarah Shaw |

**1869**

| | |
|---|---|
| Joseph Halsall | Ellen Disley |
| Edward Harrison | Rebecca Turner |
| Thomas Hewitt | Mary Berrington |
| William Horrocks | Elizabeth Forshaw |
| Joseph Jackson | Elizabeth Aspinall |
| Mark Lamb | Martha Lawson |
| Edward Langton | Elizabeth Thompson |
| John Reynolds | Ann Hilton |
| Francis Rothwell | Alice Jackson |
| John Sharrock *Wid* | Catherine Culshaw |
| Ellen Melling | William Youds |

**1870**

| | |
|---|---|
| John Blundell | Elizabeth Carr |
| Henry Bridge | Ann Baldwin *Wid* |
| William W Caunce | Mary Lewis Tyrer |
| Thomas Cheetham | Mary Webster *Wid* |
| Robert Lamb | Alice Sharrock |
| Richard Mawdsley | Rachel Riley |
| John Parr | Margaret Sawyer |
| Thomas Ruddock | Margaret Cheetham |
| Thomas Sharrock | Ann Wareing |
| William Turner | Margaret Disley |

**1871**

| | |
|---|---|
| John Baldwin | Ellen Gregson |
| Thomas Webster | Alice Moorcroft |

**1872**

| | |
|---|---|
| William Barrow | Maria Clancy |
| Henry Blundell | Mary Carrington *Wid* |
| John Forshaw | Eliza Rawlinson |
| David Livingston | Martha Hesketh |
| John Ollerton | Mary Pye |
| Luke Pye | Mary Draper |

| | |
|---|---|
| John Sharrock | Mary Barrow |
| Richard Turner | Elizabeth Wells |
| William Walker | Mary Ellen Cheetham |

**1873**

| | |
|---|---|
| James Aspinall | Ellen Cheetham |
| Robert Dutton | Ellen Mawdsley |
| Richard Gregson | Catherine Carrington |
| John Halsall | Margaret Worthington |
| Richard Hunter | Alice Lamb |
| William Lea | Elizabeth Gibbons |
| Thomas Prescott | Alice Dakin |
| Robert Robinson | Elizabeth Aspinall |
| John Watkinson | Margaret Boulton |
| William Watkinson | Elizabeth Wareing |
| William Worthington | Ann Prescott *Wid* |

**1874**

| | |
|---|---|
| Thomas Ashton | Ellen Alty |
| John Fred Blower | Eliza Dakin |
| Thomas Gibbons | Elizabeth Disley |
| Robert Howard *Wid* | Margery Spencer *Wid* |
| James Langton | Margaret Jackson |
| John Lea | Ruth Pye |
| Thomas Pemberton | Mary Jackson |
| Henry Prescott | Elizabeth Harrison |
| James Watkinson | Martha Lamb |

**1875**

| | |
|---|---|
| James Barrow | Elizabeth Disley |
| Richard Baldwin | Elizabeth Gregson |
| Thomas Baldwin | Elizabeth Taylor |
| Richard Draper | Sarah Davies |
| Joseph Halsall *Wid* | Ellen Langton |
| Holercroft Hesketh | Ellen Nelson *Wid* |
| William Langton | Ellen Tasker |
| Edward Robinson | Mary Alice Mawdsley |
| Geoffrey Sharrock | Ann Cookson |
| Edward Stringman | Ann Gore |
| Thomas Taylor *Wid* | Margaret Crank |
| Peter Tyrer | Alice Dakin |

**1876**

| | |
|---|---|
| Richard Aspinall | Ann Aspinall |
| Richard Baldwin | Elizabeth Forshaw |
| John Disley | Grace Forshaw |
| William Forshaw | Ann Tyrer |

| | |
|---|---|
| Peter Gibbons | Margaret Gibbons |
| William Gill | Elizabeth Freeman |
| Philip Glover | Ellen Forshaw |
| Robert Jackson | Mary Carrington |
| Charles Lamb | Ellen Aspinall |
| William Melling | Jane Martland |
| Thomas Thompson | Margaret Carrington |

**1877**

| | |
|---|---|
| Thomas Forshaw | Ann Barrow |
| Samuel Gregson | Alice Gregson |
| Hugh Iddon | Elizabeth Meadows |
| John Lamb *Wid* | Martha Baldwin |
| John Fred Walker | Emma Brittain |
| Margaret Gregson | Richard Watkinson |

**1878**

| | |
|---|---|
| James Ashcroft | Mary Porter |
| Henry Dakin | Martha Spencer *Wid* |
| Henry Gibbons | Elizabeth Snape |
| Peter Gibbons | Ann Spencer |
| John Hilton | Jane Baybutt |
| James Langton | Ellen Alty |
| James Lawson | Margaret Aspinall |
| Thomas Prescott | Martha Jones *Wid* |
| James Robinson | Ellen Lamb |

**1879**

| | |
|---|---|
| Thomas Deakin | Elizabeth Ann Thompson |
| George Gibbons | Jane Vickers |
| Thomas Gibbons | Mary Spencer |
| Joseph Grimshaw | Alice Carrington |
| William Lamb | Annie Hind |
| John Reynolds *Wid* | Ellen Hartley |
| William Rothwell | Mary Ellen Robinson |
| Henry Shaw | Jane Draper |

**1880**

| | |
|---|---|
| William Aspinall | Susannah Robinson |
| Thomas Cheetham | Margaret Ashton |
| William Crank | Catherine Aspinall |
| John Culshaw | Elizabeth Prescott |
| William Jackson | Ann Fishwick |
| Richard Meadows | Rebecca Lamb |
| George Thompson *Wid* | Alice Prescott *Wid* |

**1881**

| | |
|---|---|
| John Barrow | Ellen Halsall |
| Edward Culshaw | Mary Spencer |
| William Deakin | Emily Billen *Wid* |
| James Glover | Margaret Forshaw *Wid* |
| George Hesketh | Ann Taylor |
| Thomas Hind | Harriet Davies |
| William Howard | Ellen Spencer |
| Thomas Hunter | Margaret Hartley |
| Richard Jackson | Elizabeth Cheetham |
| Thomas Lamb | Elizabeth Bradley |
| Edward Prescott | Mary Martin |
| William Prescott | Margaret Langton *Wid* |
| William Pye | Ellen Meadows |
| Thomas Ruddock *Wid* | Sarah Spencer *Wid* |

**1882**

| | |
|---|---|
| Henry Alty | Jane Pilkington |
| John Ashcroft | Jane Sharrock |
| Richard Aspinall | Ellen Mather |
| James Carrington | Rachel Wood *Wid* |
| William Carrington | Ann Baldwin |
| Joseph L Deakin | Almenar Richardson |
| James Gibbons | Sarah Hornby |
| John Gibbons | Elizabeth Forshaw |
| James Grundy | Sarah Taylor |
| Roger Mawdsley | Elizabeth Ann Shaw |
| Christopher Terrell | Sarah Collins |
| Joseph Topping | Anne Prescott |

**1883**

| | |
|---|---|
| Robert Alty | Martha Harrison |
| William Carrington | Elizabeth Swift |
| Joseph Glover | Elizabeth Davison *Wid* |
| Arthur Gore | Ellen Abram |
| Elias Grimshaw | Elizabeth Blundell |
| Henry Harrison | Mary Varley |
| Peter Lamb | Sarah Jane Culshaw |
| Mary Melling | Robert Lawson |
| Martin Smith *Wid* | Ellen Halsall *Wid* |
| Thomas Varley | Elizabeth Abram |
| John Wright | Sarah Houghton |

**1884**

| | |
|---|---|
| Lawrence Almond | Margaret Culshaw |
| Henry Cheetham *Wid* | Jane Culshaw |

| | |
|---|---|
| Richard Halsall | Ann Culshaw *Wid* |
| John Howard | Ann Dakin |
| Robert Howard | Margery Spencer |
| Charles Lamb | Margaret Aspinall |
| John Harrison | Elizabeth Alty |
| John Tasker | Eleanor Gill |
| Henry Parr | Catherine Abram |
| William Plumb *Wid* | Mary Collier *Wid* |
| James Robinson | Elizabeth Dakin |
| James Robinson | Ann Ellis *Wid* |

**1885**

| | |
|---|---|
| William Blinkhorn | Ellen Harrison |
| James Ashcroft | Elizabeth Barrow |
| Thomas Ashcroft | Ellen Whittle |
| Richard Gill | Margaret Smith |
| William Gill | Hannah Lawson |
| Joseph Harrison | Ellen Huyton |
| Ralph Melling | Mary Barrow |
| Thomas Melling | Elizabeth Hornby |
| Thomas Pye | Ellen Robinson |
| James Smith | Catherine Jackson |
| Henry Spencer | Ann Duddle |
| Thomas Swift | Alice Ann Thompson |

**1886**

| | |
|---|---|
| Thomas Ashcroft | Alice Sharrock |
| John Baldwin *Wid* | Rossetta Lang *Wid* |
| James Carrington | Margaret Taylor |
| Thomas Grimshaw | Sarah Wood |
| James Halsall | Margaret Watkinson |
| Joseph Howard | Ellen Gore |
| James Lewis | Elizabeth Dakin *Wid* |
| James Watkinson | Susan Ann Baybutt |
| John Wright | Dorothy Deakin |

**1887**

| | |
|---|---|
| Thomas Berry | Jane Wareing |
| Thomas Coulton | Elizabeth Sharrock *Wid* |
| John Culshaw | Margaret Martin *Wid* |
| William Culshaw | Mary Cheetham |
| William Culshaw | Mary Culshaw |
| Thomas Gill | Margaret Alice Gibbons |
| Hugh Glover | Jane Caunce |
| Hector Parr | Margaret Tasker |
| John Sharrock | Ellen Hartley |
| William Taylor | Alice Sharman |
| William Thompson | Margaret Culshaw |
| Henry Vickers | Ellen Dutton |
| Robert Warmsley | Jane Halsall |

**1888**

| | |
|---|---|
| Thomas Ashcroft | Jane Blundell |
| George Aspinall | Mary Pardoe |
| Richard Bowen | Ann Robinson |
| Edward Cheetham | Alice Snape |
| Henry Cheetham | Mary Cheetham |
| Henry Forshaw | Mary Tasker |
| Richard Gregson | Elizabeth Robinson |
| James Robinson | Ellen Robinson |
| William Smith | Nancy Spencer |
| Joseph Stringfellow | Esther Harrison *Wid* |

**1889**

| | |
|---|---|
| Richard Carrington | Margaret George |
| Thomas Disley | Maria Sharrock |
| James Lamb | Helena Reid |
| William Joseph Lyon | Emma Gill |
| James Martland | Ellen Barrow *Wid* |
| James Mawdsley | Martha Prescott |
| Thomas Melling | Elizabeth Hornby |
| John Pedder | Ellen Robinson |
| Edward Scandle | Annie Baldwin |
| Robert Watkinson | Matilda Hartley |
| Thomas A Wilson | Ann Sharrock |

**1890**

| | |
|---|---|
| William Abram | Mary Gibbons |
| Thomas Bowen | Ann Grimshaw |
| Thomas Carrington | Elizabeth Spencer |
| William Carrington *Wid* | Mary Prescott |
| Richard Forshaw | Ann Spencer |
| John Harrison | Ellen Gore |
| James Lamb | Emma Draper |
| John Lamb | Ann Ashcroft |
| Miles Lawson | Margaret Whittle |
| James Spencer | Martha Hilton |
| Maurice Tallon *Wid* | Alice E Robinson |

**1891**

| | |
|---|---|
| Richard Deakin | Margaret Baldwin |
| William Draper | Hannah Melling |
| James Halsall | Winifred Watkinson |

| | |
|---|---|
| Thomas Halsall | Alice Yates |
| Edward Lamb | Margaret Boylan |

**1892**

| | |
|---|---|
| William Baldwin *Wid* | Elizabeth Rochford |
| Thomas Dakin | Alice Spencer |
| Henry Disley | Margaret Fairclough |
| John Eaves | Catherine Gregson |
| Thomas Halsall *Wid* | Ellen Neale *Wid* |
| Richard Meadows *Wid* | Mary Chadwick |
| John Rimmer | Mary Hartley |
| Henry Spencer | Mary Alty |
| Thomas Vickers | Jane Ashcroft |

**1893**

| | |
|---|---|
| Robert Cheetham | Elizabeth Dobson |
| John Foster | Ellen Draper |
| Thomas Foster *Wid* | Ellen Robinson *Wid* |
| Robert Gibbons | Isabella Tasker |
| James Gore | Martha Dutton |
| Robert Jackson | Sarah Ann Sharrock |
| James Lea | Jane Bentham |
| Robert Spencer | Sarah Spencer |
| Thomas Spencer | Annie Walker |
| Simeon Vickers | Mary Halsall |
| Richard Walker | Jessie Hartley |
| John Wright *Wid* | Rosa Gratton *Wid* |

**1894**

| | |
|---|---|
| James Alty | Sarah Aspinall |
| William Baldwin *Wid* | Agnes Philips |
| John Cheetham | Alice Disley |
| Henry Culshaw | Margaret Ann Langton |
| Robert Gregson | Mary Ann Cooper |
| John Charles Hatton | Catherine Lawson |
| John Marsden | Catherine Swift |
| Thomas Spencer | Alice Elizabeth Bolton |
| John Taylor *Wid* | Mary Davies *Wid* |
| James Thompson *Wid* | Susan Jackson *Wid* |

**1895**

| | |
|---|---|
| William Aspinall | Mary Robinson |
| Edward Baldwin | Margaret J Barrow |
| Thomas Gore | Margaret Parr |
| William Martland | Ellen Sharrock *Wid* |
| Thomas Stoppforth | Margaret Abram |

**1896**

| | |
|---|---|
| James Cheetham | Maria Lamb |
| James Gore | Hannah Walker |
| Peter Johnson | Jane Bell |
| John Wareing | Ellen Melling |
| John Webster | Elizabeth Gill |

**1897**

| | |
|---|---|
| Edward Baldwin | Margaret Langton |
| Hugh Collins | Mary Ellen Mather |
| Richard Dakin | Louisa Porter |
| Henry Draper | Ann Spencer |
| James Evans | Anna Gregson |
| James Evans | Anne Gregson |
| Peter Gibbons | Catherine Collins |
| Thomas Howcroft | Margaret Spencer *Wid* |
| Robert Lawson | Margaret Yates |
| William Melling | Harriet Hartley |
| Edwin Robinson | Jane Hesketh |
| Peter Ruddock | Elizabeth Cheetham |
| John Thompson | Margaret Spencer *Wid* |
| John Vickers | Elizabeth Cheetham |
| Charles Walker | Elizabeth Gore |
| John Wareing | Ellen Melling |
| William Wignall | Ellen Watkinson |

**1898**

| | |
|---|---|
| Richard Draper | Mary Gore |
| David Gill | Hannah Eaves |
| Job Gore | Margaret Melling |
| Robert Hesketh | Cecily Ann Gill |
| Edward Langton | Hannah Forshaw |
| John Mather | Elizabeth Iddon *Wid* |
| William Robinson | Ellen Prescott |
| John Rosbottom | Mary J Alty |
| Daniel Vickers | Margaret Disley |
| Henry Wright | Sarah Ellen Gore |

**1899**

| | |
|---|---|
| Thomas Baldwin | Catherine Melling |
| William Henry Lea | Martha Aspinall |
| Hector Mawdsley | Alice Hargraves |
| George Prescott | Annie Collins |
| William Sharrock | Ellen Howard *Wid* |
| John Swift | Margaret Spencer |

**1900**

| | |
|---|---|
| Thomas Alty *Wid* | Elizabeth Varley *Wid* |
| William Alty | Annie Carrington |
| James Ashcroft | Hannah Gregson |
| Richard Aspinall | Mary Walker |
| William Carrington *Wid* | Ellen Pedder *Wid* |
| John Cheetham | Hannah Howard |
| Thomas Fazakerley | Ellen Cheetham |
| George Gibbons | Cicely Collins |
| Richard Gibbons | Ellen Webster |
| Joseph Howard | Martha Huntly |
| William Henry Langton | Ellen Alty |
| James William Lawson | Alice Gore |
| William Pemberton | Elizabeth A Parkinson |
| Thomas Pye | Jane Howard |
| William Draper Pye | Margaret E Mawdsley |
| John Robinson | Hannah Davies |
| William Spencer | Jane Gibbons |
| William Robert Taylor | Ellen Gibbons |
| William Taylor | Ellen Grimshaw |
| William Vickers | Grace Parr |
| William Webster | Jane Gibbons |

**1901**

| | |
|---|---|
| Henry James Alty | Margaret Howard |
| Thomas Baldwin | Margaret Marsden |
| Edward Baybutt | Ellen Glover |
| Thomas Draper | Elizabeth Ashcroft |
| William Edmondson | Mary Lawson |
| James Marsden | Ellen Robinson |
| James Sharrock | Elizabeth Melling *Wid* |
| Thomas Spencer | Emily Deakin |
| Thomas Wareing | Hannah Alty |
| James Sharrock | Elizabeth Melling |

**1902**

| | |
|---|---|
| Richard Abram | Alice Watkinson |
| Robert Barrow | Mary Elizabeth Culshaw |
| James Draper | Jane Elizabeth Aspinall |
| Thomas Draper | Martha Watkinson |
| William Glover | Margaret Thompson |
| Thomas Meadows | Mary Ann Whittle |
| Thomas Peet | Emma Lamb |
| Walter Reynolds | Alice Prescott |

**1903**

| | |
|---|---|
| John Baldwin | Ellen Gregson |
| Henry Crowell | Margaret Watkinson |
| John Gore | Margaret Deakin |
| James Gregson *Wid* | Ellen Pye *Wid* |
| James Lewis *Wid* | Ellen Halsall *Wid* |
| Joseph Taylor | Elizabeth Carrington |
| John Wareing | Elizabeth Harrison |

**1904**

| | |
|---|---|
| William Abram | Jane Wright |
| Edward Baldwin | Margaret Dutton |
| Richard Gibbons | Elizabeth Gregson |
| John Langton | Winifred Dutton |
| John Norris | Mary Ashcroft |
| Peter Porter | Grace Vickers *Wid* |
| Thomas Robinson | Annie Spencer |

**1905**

| | |
|---|---|
| Richard Houghton | Ann Cheetham |
| Richard Halsall | Elizabeth Culshaw *Wid* |
| William Lamb *Wid* | Mary Ann Houghton *Wid* |
| George Meadows | Elizabeth Hesketh |
| Henry Melling | Mary Alice Watkinson |
| Edward Spencer | Elizabeth E Marshall |
| John Ollerton | Sarah Thompson |
| Ann Howard | Charles George Riley |

**1906**

| | |
|---|---|
| William Barrow | Catherine Alty |
| Henry Dawson | Maria Glover |
| James Gore | Sarah Varley |
| William Lamb | Francess Ellen Price |
| John Parr | Margaret Watkinson |
| Richard Parr | Elizabeth Rosbottom |

**1907**

| | |
|---|---|
| Adam Ashcroft | Elizabeth Deakin |
| William Ashcroft | Sarah Ann Twigg |
| William Baldwin | Catherine Jackson |
| William Gore | Eleanor Tasker |
| Edward Lawson | Alice Barrow |
| Hector Mawdsley | Ellen Pye |
| Jeffery Wareing | Francess Robinson |
| Henry Woodcock | Martha Jackson |

**1908**

Henry Alty — Mary Ashcroft
John Ashcroft — Elizabeth Thompson
John Blundell — Ellen Alice Gibbons
Richard Forshaw — Sarah Elizabeth Howard
William Gibbons — Ellen Alty
William Halsall — Margaret Aspinall
William Hartley — Mary Glover
John Lamb *Wid* — Ellen Hewitt *Wid*
John Lamb *Wid* — Helen Hewitt *Wid*
James Webster — Margaret Ruddock
Richard Webster — Elizabeth Tyrer

**1909**

Robert Alty — Sarah Jane Langton
Richard Baldwin — Mary Hewitt
William Baldwin — Mary Culshaw
John Fairhurst — Alice Gore
Henry Gibbons — Cicely Gibbons *Wid*
William Gibbons — Catherine Halsall
Job Howard — Marian Glover
Thomas Ruddock *Wid* — Cicely Johnson *Wid*

**1910**

Henry Ashton — Jane Blinkhorn
Thomas Bowen — Margaret Lamb
William Deakin — Mary Gibbons
William Langton — Alice Blinkhorn
John Robert Thompson — Elizabeth Ashcroft

**1911**

John Gibbons — Ellen Woodcock
Edward Hesketh — Susan Helen Gill
Daniel Marsden — Elizabeth Wilkinson
Henry Prescott — Catherine Cheetham
Henry Spencer — Rebecca Watkinson
William Spencer — Annie Wignall
Robert Varley — Ellen Rothwell

**1912**

James Barrow — Jane Alty
Henry Forshaw — Elizabeth Jane Ashcroft
Peter Gibbons — Hannah Thompson
Richard Halsall — Mary Cheetham
Thomas Jackson *Wid* — Ellen Lamb *Wid*
Ellen Lamb *Wid* — Thomas Jackson *Wid*

Henry Lawson — Mary Georgeson
James McGrath — Elizabeth Varley
William Melling — Mary Draper

**1913**

John Baldwin — Margaret Gibbons
Arthur Gore — Ann Hesketh
Robert Howard — Elizabeth Mawdsley
John Harwood — Elizabeth Thompson
William Lyon — Ann Smith
James Parr — Ruth Baldwin
Thomas Webster — Mary Swift

**1914**

Adam Ashcroft — Edith Watkinson
Henry Glover — Dorothy Wright
James Hilton — Ann Carrington
Richard Jackson — Elizabeth Ellen Foster
Thomas Parr — Margaret Ellen Gibbons
William Smith Kirby — Elizabeth Forshaw
John Warmsley — Ellen Howard

**1915**

John Forshaw — Sarah Sutton
William Forshaw — Margaret Mawdsley
Richard Gibbons — Catherine Cheetham
Henry Harrison — Ellen Watkinson
John Lamb — Martha Forshaw
George W Ollerton — Jane Rockcliffe
James Vickers — Emma Gill
James Watkinson — Margaret Watkinson

**1916**

Richard Deakin — June Martin
James Forshaw — Ellen Draper
Edward Glover — Amy Robina Peers
Richard Jackson — Jane Cheetham *Wid*
Charles Lamb — Alice Ashcroft
Richard Lamb — Elizabeth Ellen Wright

**1917**

Richard Prescott — Janey Gibbons
John Pye — Edith Forshaw

**1918**

Henry Cheetham *Wid* — Margaret Howcroft *Wid*
James Lamb — Cissie Lawson
Miles Lamb — Ellen Carrington

John Lawson — Elizabeth Kerr
Luke Pye — Ellen Lamb

**1919**

John Cheetham — Mary Edwardson
Richard Forshaw — Ellen Gibbons *Wid*
Peter Gibbons — Margaret Cheetham
William Gibbons *Wid* — Jane Glover *Wid*
Thomas Halsall — Margaret Hartley
James Harrison — Winifred Watkinson
Robert Hewitt — Edith Forrest
Robert Howard — Mary Watkinson
Isaac Lamb — Margaret Stringman
Thomas Lamb — Dorothy Glover
William Lamb — Mary Ann Lamb
Richard Parr — Bessie Bradley
John William Varley — Elizabeth Ann Gibbons
Jacob Walker — Elizabeth Smith
Allen John Williams — Isobella Deakin

**1920**

Robert Alty — Mary Alice Forshaw
Richard Ashcroft — Mary Forshaw
Thomas Draper — Elizabeth Forshaw
John Grimshaw — Sarah Webster
John Vickers — Mary Ann Lewis

**1921**

Peter Ashcroft — Elizabeth McCann *Wid*
William Baldwin — Jane Almond
Charles Cheetham — Jane Martland
James Halsall — Margaret Tasker

**1922**

Robert Blinkhorn — Winifred Dutton
William Gibbons — Mary Rosbottom
Stephen Lamb — Sarah Ann Fazakerley
John Rimmer Wright — Jane Webster
John Robert Wright — Jane Webster

**1923**

Finch Henry Blundell — Nancy Gibbons
James Deakin — Prudence Ollerton
William Draper — Margaret Ann Forshaw
Richard Watkinson — Cecily Smith

**1924**

Stephen Aspinall — Jane Spencer

William Deakin — Mary Hartley *Wid*
Arthur James Gore — Ellen Blinkhorn
William Gore — Martha Gore
William Lamb — Margaret Forshaw

**1925**

Richard Abram — Jane Elizabeth Barrow
John Draper — Ann Bowen
Thomas Forshaw — Elizabeth Gaskell
Richard Glover — Ellen Robinson
Charles Lamb — Catherine Marsden
John Pedder — Catherine Watkinson
Robert Watkinson — Elizabeth Spencer

**1926**

Peter Gibbons — Mary Ellen Rimmer

**1927**

James Draper — Maria Sharrock
Thomas Forshaw — Elizabeth Ann Smith
James Langton — Elizabeth Gregson

**1928**

Robert Gregson — Margaret Smith Forshaw
Robert Hesketh — Ann Jane Sharrock

**1929**

Richard Forshaw — Ann Coulton

**1930**

Ellen Disley — William Forshaw
William Forshaw — Ellen Disley
George Gibbons — Margaret Fyles
William Gregson — Bertha Harrison

**1931**

Albert Cheetham — Mary E Pye

**1935**

Henry Deakin — Sarah Ann Holford

A landmine dropped by the German Luftwaffe during an air raid on Liverpool in 1942 breaching the canal by the Bankhall loading cradle. It caused a stoppage to all canal traffic in and out of Liverpool for eight weeks.

Boats owned by John Parke and Sons Ltd, each loaded with approximately 60 tonnes of coal at the Bankhall railway loading platform a mile away, waiting to be discharged by elevator buckets at Liverpool's Athol Street gasworks. 1944.
Up until about 1945 the boats were towed by horses; they were replaced by small, steam-driven tugboats. The days of the workhorse were coming to an end.

Tate & Lyle discharging berths between Burlington and Chisenhale Street bridges, and the length of canal where Liverpool urchins who lived in the Vauxhall area used to swim at times when the factory was closed, i.e. on Saturday afternoons and more especially on Sundays. They swam in the canal water made warm by discharged boiler water used in the manufacture of sugar. The barges were the diving-off platforms. It was how the author learned to swim.

Henry Cheetham and his second wife Margaret (sitting) with Bill Lee (extreme left) and wife Elizabeth listening to the launching of the liner Queen Mary, while berthed at the Tate & Lyle refinery, waiting to discharge a cargo of coal brought by horse tow from the Wigan coalfields. 1936.

The Lawson family having some 'snap' (food and drink) at Tate & Lyles.

Liverpool Corporation's refuse yard (Muck Quay) in Chisenhale Street where, after discharging coal at Tate & Lyle's next door, barge captains used to seek a load of horse manure, brought in off the street by special horse carts, to take up country to farmers' fields en route to the Wigan coalfields. It was regarded as a 'load back' with extra tonnable money due, instead of travelling to Wigan empty. This part of the canal, parallel to Pall Mall, has now been filled in.

A steam-driven boat moored alongside a fly-boat tow, loading bales of wool at Sandhills warehouse, Liverpool, destined for the Lancashire and Yorkshire cotton mills. 1900.

One of Canal Transport's last diesel-driven steel-plated boats to be built before the eventual closure of the canal to commercial traffic in the early 1960s. Boat 'Everton' passing under the Litherland electrically operated lift bridge. Her captain was Tom Abram in the 1950s. The operator's house and the hut can be seen, where James Lovelady pressed the buttons to lift and lower the bridge. Now replaced with a modern flyover.

Litherland bridge in 1900 when it was a manually pushed 'off and on' bridge. The ancient, iron walk-over bridge is still serving pedestrians today.

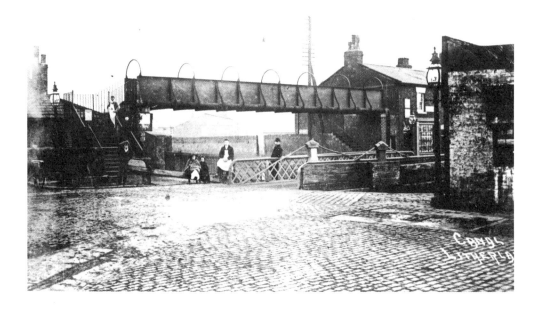

A boat belonging to Bootle Corporation preparing for a tug-towed outing to Aintree with Bootle residents on board. The barge was normally used for carrying incinerated household refuse to a tipping site in Melling, ten miles north of Bootle. The boat had been specially cleaned for the occasion. The author's brother, 'Captain' Richard Houghton (in shirt sleeves, on the bow deck), Litherland Road bridge and 'King Dicks' pub in the background.

A recent photograph of Litherland Road bridge with Bootle's coat of arms painted in the centre and William's toffee works' chimney that stood for over 80 years (now demolished). The overgrown bushes in front of the pub is the land on which stood Boatmen's gas-lighted cottages and the beginning of the original Bootle Village, where the author was born.

'King Dicks' public house was once a favourite watering hole for many generations of bargees while they were tied up at Bootle gasworks, waiting to discharge cargoes of coal for furnaces.

Linacre Lane and Linacre Village of Bootle-cum-Linacre, winter of 1890. Note the corner shop on Litherland Road, a gas lamp and the Linacre public house on the canal bridge (left of picture) which is still selling beer to this day. Also a corporation 'muck cart' with its two horses standing eating provender from nosebags.

Bootle-cum-Linacre gasworks where once, and for many years, there were always dozens of lined-up coal-laden barges berthed. Totalling thousands of tonnes, coal was transported from the colliery by railway wagons to Bankhall Sidings, then loaded into boats and towed by horses to both Bootle and Liverpool gasworks. All of which are no more.

A steeplechaser participating in the 1948 Grand National at Aintree racecourse, failing to turn left at the 'canal turn' and finishing up in the canal itself, with a despondent Tim Malony, the jockey, standing on the canal bank with a policeman.

'Halsall Length' near Ormskirk where the first sod was cut, with solid rock underneath, at the commencement of the making of the Leeds to Liverpool Canal in 1770. One gang of men ('navvies' for navigational) commenced digging with spades and barrows in the direction of Liverpool, while another dug in the direction of Wigan and eventually across the Pennine Chain and all the way to the city of Leeds, a final distance of 127 1/4 miles, necessitating the construction of scores of locks and bridges on the way.

Motor boat and towed dummy boat 'Bruno' approaching Dean Lock, Gathurst, Wigan, and the newly completed M6 motorway flyover which hastened the closure of the canal. The motor boat would be laden with about 50 tonnes of coal and the tow, which had a greater overall length, with approximately 65 tonnes, destined for the gasworks in Liverpool. It was a round trip which took two or three days (Liverpool to Wigan and back) at a speed of approximately three miles an hour.

The author, and mate of Richard William's boat 'Progress', at the tiller steering her at Downholland, near Ormskirk, in 1942 en route to Liverpool. The captain was James (Jem) Halsall who lived in a canalside cottage at Haskayne Bridge, opposite the 'Ship Inn' public house. The cargo was loaded at the Garswood Hall loading cradle 'on the moss', Wigan, and destined for the Tate & Lyle sugar refinery in Liverpool.

The ex-Ainscough's grain-carrying 14ft-wide iron boat 'Ambush', once used for transporting grain from Birkenhead, across the River Mersey, to their flour mill at Burscough. Now in private ownership being used as a floating restaurant, berthed at Burscough Bridge among many narrow pleasure boats from other canals.

The comparatively new steel-plated boat 'Everton', berthed at Burscough in the 1950s. Captain Tom Abram.

Coal-carrying timber-built motorboat 'Margaret' berthed on the towpath side at Burscough Bridge. The owners were Richard Williams and Sons, 24 Chapel Street, Liverpool, nicknamed 'Dicky Billies'. In the 1940s its crew comprised the brothers Dick and Harry Gibbons of Victoria Street, Burscough, sons of Thomas Gibbons. The raised bow cabin top was only added sometime in the late 1950s. Her carrying capacity was approximately 50 tonnes.

Mrs Bridge of Burscough, wife, boat's mate, and mother of some fine Burscough boatmen. Note dog kennel and dog on the stern deck and ventilation 'lid'.

H&R Ainscough's grain-carrying iron boat 'Viktoria' which was towed across the River Mersey to Birkenhead Mills by river tug-boat, to load the grain for the Burscough Mills. The winch on her bow deck was for the crew to winch across the Liverpool Stanley Dock to Stanley Locks to gain access to and from the Leeds and Liverpool Canal.

One of Ben Walls' dummy boats tied up opposite the Canal Company premises.

The author's father, Dick 'Ranty' Houghton wheeling out a boatload of horse manure into a farmer's field at Tarleton near Preston on the Rufford line of the canal. The manure was loaded at the Liverpool refuse depot in Chisenhale Street, Liverpool. The boat 'Ben' was owned by William Knowles and Son of Carruthers Street, Liverpool, hay and straw merchants, who for many years supplied the fodder to boatmen for their horses. There was also a knacker's yard in the same street which always gave off obnoxious smells.

Canal Company banksmen breaking ice during the long freeze in 1947. Tom Draper, in clogs and with cigarette, looking on.

Tom Carrington and wife 'tied up' at Burscough Bridge. Known on the canal as 'Tommy Nine Toes' after being trod on by his own horse.

At Burscough a young Daniel Parr with boat horse. Lavery's cake factory in the background.

Tom Lamb from New Lane canalside houses with boat horse. Note the swingletree on the horse's tack, across its rear, for hooking the towrope on.

Some of the author's many ancestors, the Cheethams, gathered aboard the John Parke-owned boat 'Plato' at Burscough Bridge, 1910. A good many of them were born in boat cabins.
'Plato' finished its days as a non-residential barge carrying coal from the Bankhall loading cradle to gasworks at Liverpool and Bootle.

More Burscough boatmen in their 'Sunday best', wearing boots instead of the usual clogs.

The author aged three with grandmother Jane Cheetham, nee Culshaw, 66, ex-boatwoman, sitting knitting a boatman's 'gansey' outside her parlour window in Litherland Road, Bootle Village, 1927. She is now interred, along with many of the Cheetham family, in St John the Baptist churchyard at Burscough Bridge.

Tom Baybutt (3rd from the left) with brother boatmen, on board boat 'Don' at New Lane, Burscough, posing for the camera. Tom was the captain of Canal Transport's iron boat 'Irwell' during the 1930s and '40s.

Rear view of the now retired Ainscough's steel-plated boat 'Ambush', with the renamed 'Packet House' pub in the background, now the 'Lord Nelson'.

The 'Pride of Sefton' owned by Sefton Council and used for taking handicapped people on canal trips. Berthed at the Ship Inn bridge, Haskayne, 1988.

Crabtree swing bridge, Burscough, 1994.

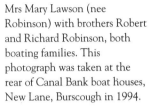

Mrs Mary Lawson (nee Robinson) with brothers Robert and Richard Robinson, both boating families. This photograph was taken at the rear of Canal Bank boat houses, New Lane, Burscough in 1994.

Houses built on the canalside in the 1880s especially for boating families at New Lane, Burscough. Today, many of the houses have been modernised to a great extent and are still occupied by the same families, though a new generation following other occupations, some of whom are posing for the camera outside the birthplace of the author's mother, Anne Cheetham.

'The Farmers Arms', New Lane swing bridge. Once the haunt of boatmen past.

Canal cottages and boat families at Newburgh, Parbold, about 1920.　　H & R Ainscough's horse boat leaving Appley Lock bound for Wigan, 1935.

Today's Parbold Mill bridge, updated from a narrow humpty-backed one to facilitate the increased traffic requirements. A popular berthing spot for converted, 'lived-in' narrow boats.

One of the 125 milestones positioned on the towpath along the canal. This particular one is at Wigan.

The one-time loading cradle at Crook near Wigan, known locally as 'John Pit'. The coal came from Crook Hall colliery nearby.

Canal Transport's warehouse at Wigan when it was fully operational in the 1940s with the well-known cotton mill landmark in the background. A fully-loaded horse-drawn coal boat, en route to Liverpool, can be seen being pulled by the horse with a white blaze on its face, as it is about to climb the rise on the towpath, which in fact is the part known as 'Wigan Pier'. A boatman can just be seen leading the horse.

Wigan depot, lying still and quiet in between the commercial closure of the canal and its transformation into a tourist attraction.

A Canal Transport iron boat with crew sitting on the bow deck at Wigan warehouse. Boat 'Mersey' berthed ahead during the war in 1942. The raised towpath near the top of the picture is the factual structure known as Wigan Pier, the butt of many music hall jokes in days gone by.

Boat 'Mary Jane' with owner James Mawdsley standing on the stern deck (extreme left) with his sons. Colliery women workers also in attendance at the coal cradle at the 12th lock of Wigan's 21 locks. Coal delivered by rail from Rose Bank colliery.

Horse-drawn boat at Greenberfield lock with its two-sided towing masts for when the towpath changes over. Its cargo consisted of bales of wool heading from Liverpool berthed ships to Yorkshire cotton-spinning mills.

Boat 'Mu' and crew. The bike was used for 'going ahead' to manually swing wooden road bridges off and on again, and to prepare locks for entering by filling or emptying (dropping) them, the object was to expedite the operation.

Steam packets and dummy boats held up for a week at Eanham near Blackburn in 1919 because of drought and the low depth of the canal.

Bingley five-rise locks, Yorkshire.

More melodian playing boatmen
somewhere in Yorkshire.

Tom Bowen, nicknamed 'Old Shiney', who lived with his wife Ann at Appley Lock Cottages, and where he stabled his boat horse at the rear. Ashurst Beacon in the top background.

Unloading bales of wool at Church.

Fly-boats delayed at Gargrave because of low water levels, 1930.

Tom Bowen and his boat laden with 35 tonnes of crated machinery being pulled along by Ben, the horse, at Barnoldswick. Son Tom sitting on the stern deck rail, playing a melodian.

Ex-Canal Transport motor boat 'Bacup' being used as a bank maintenance boat by the Canal Company, after her cargo-carrying days.

Boat 'Bacup' now restored to her former working livery at the boat museum, Ellesmere Port, Cheshire. The author is standing beside her, 1994.

Norman Walls, son of Ben Walls, boat owner, later a director of Canal Transport after selling his boats to them and amalgamating.

Some of my country cousins, the Cheethams, whose male members are still working on the Leeds and Liverpool canal at Skipton, employed as banksmen. Left to right: Margaret, Susan, Pauline and David. Seated are Vera and Vincent, 1994.

Fly boats held up at Gargrave
locks because of drought, 1930.

An unladen horse boat leaving
Apperley Lock in Yorkshire
with a loaded one waiting to
enter and climb to the next
level. (Apperley Lock not to be
confused with Appley Lock near
Wigan, Lancashire, which is the
first lock encountered from
Liverpool.)

The canal basin and warehouse at Shipley, specially built for the
woolen trade. Motor boat 'Tweed' and dummy boat 'Omega' both
laden with bulk bales of wool, the latter probably having been towed by
'Tweed' from Liverpool. Note a group of boatmen talking to each
other.

The Canal Company's steamboat '40' with the banksmen dressed in the traditional brown corduroy trousers, clogs and dark navy blue 'gansey' (for Guernsey wool).

A newly-built 14ft-wide dummy boat almost ready for launching, on the stocks at the Canal Company's boatyard, Burnley.

Canal Transport's Manchester Road depot, Burnley. A hive of activity in 1910.

Canal Transport's 'Wharfe' jammed between lock gates caused by a piece of driftwood wedged behind the gate and the lock wall.

'Kebbing' for coal spillage on the bottom of the canal.

The Canal Company's steam-driven 'Waterwitch', used for transporting executives or inspection tours.

At Johnson's Hillock near Blackburn in 1926. Baby Richard Watkinson with his mother walking the towpath for a bit of exercise. Big brother John is leading the horse while it eats a bucket of provender. Father James is steering the boat.

A steam-driven boat on the Leigh cut carrying coal from Wigan to Manchester power station.

'Jumbo' belonging to Crook and Thompson. Mrs Hilda Watkinson, boat's mate, sitting on the engine house top, 1950.

Mrs Hilda Watkinson, nee Foster, living in retirement alongside the canal at Burnley. Hilda was born at No. 1 Ring O' Bells boat houses near Ormskirk, in 1905.

Coal-laden boat 'Susan' at Burnley wharfe, destination Blackburn electricity works, 1940.

A young Leslie Mitchell of the BBC interviewing boatmen Jim Mailey and Bill Pemberton in their Sunday best, at Burnley wharfe, 1942.

A sunken, fully-laden coal boat at Burnley, 1930.

A Burscough boatman teaching women (recruited under a government scheme during the 1939-45 war years because of the shortage of men) how to splice a rope. the women were quickly nicknamed 'budgies'. The idea was not a great success, as boatmen used to say: "boating is a job you have to be born to". Looking on is Ben Walls, Director of Canal Transport.

The author (right) with publisher Tom Morley and boatyard shop proprietor Mrs Marie Moore, wife of Douglas Moore of Doug Moore Ltd (Boatbuilders), Barnoldswick, Lancashire, 1993. Now a popular berthing place for leisure craft, especially in the summer months.